SNIPER TRADING WORKBOOK

WILEY TRADING

SNIPER TRADING WORKBOOK

**Step-by-Step Exercises
to Help You Master Sniper Trading**

George Angell

JOHN WILEY & SONS, INC.

Published by John Wiley & Sons, Inc., New York.
Published simultaneously in Canada.

This publication is designed to provide accurate and authoritative information in regard to the subject matter covered. It is sold with the understanding that the publisher is not engaged in rendering professional services. If professional advice or other expert assistance is required, the services of a competent professional person should be sought.

Library of Congress Cataloging-in-Publication Data:

ISBN 0-471-39423-8

10 9 8 7 6 5 4 3 2 1

Contents

Preface

This study guide is designed to be used with *Sniper Trading.* All the formulas and strategies covered here are outlined in that text. Whenever possible, I've tried to present examples that are realistic and likely to occur during the normal course of trading. Please note that this material is designed to complement, not substitute for, the textbook.

While the formulas are cut-and-dry, some of the accompanying material is interpretative in nature. For this reason, you may arrive at more than one answer for some of the questions. Do not let this frustrate you; the market is complex and does not always offer an easy answer. The sooner you recognize this complexity and integrate it into your trading, the better off you will be.

I've tried to pose a question and suggest a possible solution within the same chapter. This is so you won't have to flip back and forth as you move through the text. The chapters are designed to stand by themselves, enabling you to tackle one strategy before moving on to another one.

1

Taylor's Contribution to Technical Analysis: The Book Method

George Douglas Taylor's contribution to technical analysis cannot be underestimated. He believed in measuring both market rallies and declines, and then averaging the numbers to arrive at some approximation of what should occur on the next trading day. He called this the "Book Method." I later incorporated these numbers into my LSS 3-Day Cycle Method, adding an additional formula that I called the Trend Reaction Numbers. These same numbers were later called the LSS Pivot Buy and Sell Numbers. Leaving aside this additional formula, let's first look at Taylor's original four key numbers—the rally, the decline, the buying high, and the buying under.

Questions

1. What is the rally number and what does it measure?

2. What is the decline number and what does it measure?

3. What is the buying high number and what does it measure?

4. What is the buying under number and what does it measure?

Answers

1. The rally number measures how far the market rallies from one day to another. It is the difference between today's high (the last completed day's high) and the previous day's low. Accordingly, if today's high is 1274.00 and the previous day's low is 1231.00, the difference of 43.00 points is the rally number. If one is trading U.S. Treasury bonds and today's high (after the close) is 105-18 and the prior day's low is 104-30, the rally would be the difference, or $^{20}\!/_{32}$. This number tells us that on this particular two-day period, the market rallied $^{20}\!/_{32}$ in price. We might use this information to determine how far above today's low price the bond market might rally tomorrow. Hence, assuming we are going to use the $^{20}\!/_{32}$ number, with a low today of, let's say, 104-19, we can estimate a rally of approximately $^{20}\!/_{32}$, or a high of 105-07 ($104^{19}\!/_{32} + {}^{20}\!/_{32} = 105^{7}\!/_{32}$).

2. The decline number measures how far on average the market tends to decline from a prior day's high to today's low. If yesterday's high was 1294.00 and today's low is 1286.00, the decline is 8.00 points. Let's say today's high is 1323.00. Given an 8.00-point average decline, what can we expect for tomorrow's low? The answer is 1315.00, or 8 points lower, based on

just one day's reading. In an actual example, we would average several declines. Let's say you are trading bonds and you arrive at a decline of 1-17. You would then subtract this number from a previous day's high to arrive at a possible low or support on the following day. Let's assume the prior day's high was $105^{17}\!/_{32}$. By subtracting the decline number, you would arrive at an answer of 104-00.

3. The buying high number measures how far above the prior day's high the market traded today (the day just finished). In a rising market, you will have positive buying high numbers. In a declining market (with lower tops), you will have negative numbers. The formula for buying high is today's high minus yesterday's high. So if today's high is 1249.00 and yesterday's high was 1243.00, the difference is 6.00 points, the buying high number. If we want to assume the same buying high number will prevail tomorrow, we simply add on the buying high to today's high. This will give us a target of 1255.00 (1249.00 today's high + 6.00 buying high = 1255.00). Let's say you are trading the U.S. Treasury bonds. Today's high is 103-11 and yesterday's high was 102-17. Obviously, the market has been rising rapidly, as reflected in a buying high of $^{26}\!/_{32}$. If the market continues to rise at this rate tomorrow, the buying high would give us a target top of 104-05 (103-11 today's high + $^{26}\!/_{32}$ = 104-05).

4. The buying under number measures how far today's low traded under yesterday's low. Hence, for a positive number to occur in the buying under, you must have a lower low today, since the calculation is yesterday's low minus today's low. A rising market will give you a negative number for the buying under. Let's say yesterday's low was 1260.00 and today's low was 1267.00. The market has been rising. This will give you a negative number of −6.00 for the buying under. When you go to *subtract*

this number from today's low of 1267.00, you will arrive at a higher number—namely 1274.00—since two negatives added together result in an addition. An easier example is when yesterday's low was, let's say, 1077.00, and today's low is 1075.00. The difference is 2.00 points. Using the buying under to generate a new low tomorrow will result in 1073.00 as the target low (1075.00 today's low − 2.00 buying under = 1073.00).

2

The Buy and Sell Envelopes: Measuring Support Resistance

Among the many uses of Taylor's numbers is the creation of the buy and sell envelopes. These are the key support and resistance numbers that traders use for short-term buying and selling. They also serve another purpose: range prediction. The numbers can be averaged to determine what tomorrow's range should look like. Once the market has opened and traded awhile, this range can be superimposed on the market to predict the day's high or low.

Questions

1. What are the components of the buy envelope?

2. What are the components of the sell envelope?

Answers

1. The buy envelope consists of the following four numbers: the average of the last three decline numbers subtracted from the last high; the average of the last three buying under numbers subtracted from the last low; the last low; and the Trend Reaction Buy Number (the LSS Pivotal Day *Sell* Number).

2. The sell envelope consists of the following four numbers: the average of the last three rally numbers added to the last low; the average of the last three buying high numbers added to the last high; the last high; and the Trend Reaction Sell Number (the LSS Pivotal Day *Buy* Number).

3

The LSS Pivotal Buy and Sell Numbers: The Trend Reaction Numbers

---

This is a simple formula that serves two seemingly contradictory purposes. On the one hand, this formula creates a buy and sell number that proves useful when the market is without a trend; on the other, the two numbers can be reversed and used as breakout points in a trend-following system.

Question

What is the formula for the LSS Pivotal Buy and Sell Numbers?

Answer

The formula for the LSS Pivotal Buy and Sell Numbers (Trend Reaction Numbers) is as follows:

$$\frac{High + Low + Close}{3} = X$$

$$2X - High = \text{LSS pivotal } sell \text{ (trend reaction buy)}$$

$$2X - Low = \text{LSS pivotal } buy \text{ (trend reaction sell)}$$

Note that the low number serves as a support when constructing the LSS envelope, but serves as a breakout sell number when the market is trending. The reverse is also true for the higher number, which is a resistance when the market is choppy, but serves as a breakout number when the market wants to trend higher. These two uses of the numbers are not contradictory, since the notion of the support becoming the resistance—and vice versa—is an accepted concept in technical analysis.

4

Putting Numbers on Support and Resistance: An Example Using a Hypothetical 5-Day Period

Creating the buy and sell envelopes is a relatively simple task. The challenge comes in interpreting the results. In the following example, the reader is asked to take five days of data and create the envelopes.

Question

Taking the following five days of data, how do you create both the buy and sell envelopes and the buy and sell numbers for the next trading day?

Day	High	Low	Close
1	1125.50	1100.00	1110.00
2	1121.00	1097.70	1121.00
3	1117.20	1103.90	1103.90
4	1097.20	1084.60	1088.50
5	1074.30	1042.00	1063.50

Answer

Starting with the simplest observation first, take note of the last high and low, 1074.30 and 1042.00. These will be entered into the sell and buy envelopes, respectively. That leaves three additional numbers for each envelope. Let's start with the trend reaction numbers:

$$\frac{1074.30 \text{ (high)} + 1042.00 \text{ (low)} + 1063.50 \text{ (close)}}{3} = X$$

$$X = 1059.90$$

Therefore, $2X = 2119.80$

$$2119.80 - 1074.30 \text{ (high)} = 1045.50 \text{ (Buy Number)}$$

$$2119.80 - 1042.00 \text{ (low)} = 1077.80 \text{ (Sell Number)}$$

We now have another set of numbers for our envelopes.

This leaves the calculations for the buying high and rally numbers for the sell envelope and the buying under and decline numbers for the buy envelope. Let's start with the calculations for the rally number. We know that on the past three days, the market has rallied the following amounts:

Day		Rally
1	19.50	(1117.20 − 1097.70 = 19.50)
2	−6.70	(1097.20 − 1103.90 = −6.70)*
3	−10.30	(1074.30 − 1084.60 = −10.30)*

*Note: Because the next day's high was below the previous day's low, this resulted in a negative number. This will happen when the market is breaking hard.

Average of last three declines = +.80

Last low + average rally = rally number

1042.00 + .80 = 1042.80 (rally number)

Now let's turn to the buying high number. Here we are comparing high to high. Since the market was declining, these will be negative numbers, as follows:

Day		Buying High
1	−3.80	(1117.20 − 1121.00 = −3.80)
2	−20.00	(1097.20 − 1117.20 = −20.00)
3	−22.90	(1074.30 − 1097.20 = −22.90)

The average of these three buying high numbers is −15.50.

Since the previous high was 1074.30 and the buying high number is *added* to that number, the result is 1058.80 [1074.30 +

(−15.50) = 1058.80]. We now have all the numbers we need for the selling envelope.

For the buying envelope, we need two additional numbers, the average decline number and the buying under number. First, let's look at the average decline. Since the market has been breaking, we can look for large positive numbers in this column. The last three declines would appear as follows:

Day		*Decline*	
1	17.10	(1121.00 − 1103.90 = 17.10)
2	32.60	(1117.20 − 1084.60 = 32.60)
3	55.20	(1097.20 − 1042.00 = 55.20)

We now average these three declines and come up with 35.00 points. This is the average decline over the past three days. We subtract this number from the last high to arrive at the decline number. Hence: 1074.30 (last high) − 35.00 (average three-day decline) = 1039.30.

This leaves us with the buying under number. We want to know how far, on average, the last low exceeded the low on the prior day. In our example, we'll have one negative number and two positive numbers in this category, since the low three days back was higher than the previous low. On the two prior days, however, the market was breaking fast, resulting in positive numbers as follows:

Day		*Buying Under*	
1	−6.20	(1097.70 − 1103.90 = −6.20)
2	19.30	(1103.90 − 1084.60 = 19.30)
3	42.60	(1084.60 − 1042.00 = 42.60)

Now you average these three numbers and arrive at an average for the buying under of 18.50. You then subtract this number from the last low of 1042.00. The result is 1023.50. You now have all the numbers you need for both the buy envelope and the sell envelope. A final calculation involves averaging each of the two envelopes and coming up with a buy and a sell number as shown.

Sell Envelope

1077.80	Trend Reaction	
1064.30	Last High	
1058.80	Buying High	
1042.80	Rally	Sell Number = 1063.40

Buy Envelope

1045.50	Trend Reaction	
1042.00	Last High	
1039.30	Decline	
1023.50	Buying Under	Sell Number = 1037.60

The final calculation is the range, the difference between the buy and sell numbers. This amounts to 25.80 points (1063.40 sell number − 1037.60 buy number = 25.80).

5

The Early Range and the Anticipated Range

Once the market has traded for approximately 30 minutes to one hour, it creates an early range. Because the probabilities favor one side of this range being the actual high or low of the day, the anticipated range can be added to the early low, or subtracted from the early high, to create a target top or bottom.

Question

Assume the day's buy number is 1206.00 and the sell number is 1244.00. If the early high is 1234.30 and the early low is 1217.00, what will be the target top and bottom?

Answer

The range you expect on the day is 38.00 points, the difference between the buy and sell number (1244.00 − 1206.00 = 38.00). The early range is 17.30 points (1234.30 − 1217.00 = 17.30). By adding the anticipated range to the early low, you reach an anticipated top (or sell) number. By subtracting the anticipated range from the early high, you reach an anticipated bottom (or buy) number. Note that it is extremely unlikely that both numbers will be hit. The probabilities do favor, however, one of the numbers being near the high or the low of the day. In this example, the target top is 1255.00 (1217.00 early low + 36.00 anticipated range = 1255.00 anticipated top). The target bottom is 1196.30 (1234.30 early high − 38.00 anticipated range = 1196.30 anticipated bottom).

6

Bond Calculations

Many people have problems with the math when it comes to doing calculations with the bonds. Do I convert the 32nds to decimals? Once you arrive at a number with a decimal, how do you convert back? Consider the following dilemma.

Question

At the end of today's trading, the September U.S. Treasury bond contract had the following range:

$$High = 101\text{-}22$$

$$Low = 100\text{-}24$$

$$Close = 100\text{-}30$$

What are tomorrow's trend reaction buy and sell numbers?

Answer

This is a relatively straightforward problem. First, you need to know the formula for the trend reaction numbers:

$$\frac{High + Low + Close}{3} = X$$

$$2X - High = Buy \text{ (LSS pivot sell) number}$$

$$2X - Low = Sell \text{ (LSS pivot buy) number}$$

Next, you need to convert the 32nds as follows:

$$101\text{-}22 = 101 \times 32 = 3232 + 22 = 3254$$

$$100\text{-}24 = 100 \times 32 = 3200 + 24 = 3224$$

$$100\text{-}30 = 100 \times 32 = 3200 + 30 = 3230$$

Now, do the math:

$$\frac{3254 + 3224 + 3230}{3} = \frac{9708}{3} = 3236 = X$$

Therefore, $2X = (3236 \times 2) = 6472$

$6472\ (2X) - 3254\ (\text{high}) = 3218$

$6472\ (2X) - 3224\ (\text{low}) = 3248$

Now it is simply a matter of converting back to 32nds.

$$100 \times 32 = 3200$$

Therefore, $3218 - 3200 = 18$

The buy number is 100-18.

$$101 \times 32 = 3232$$

Therefore, $3248 - 3232 = 16$

The sell number is 101-16.

You might make a list of the round numbers of the 32nd intervals. For example:

$$103\text{-}00 = 3296$$

$$102\text{-}00 = 3264$$

$$101\text{-}00 = 3232$$

$$100\text{-}00 = 3200$$

$$99\text{-}00 = 3168$$

$$98\text{-}00 = 3136$$

Anytime you arrive at a number that falls within one of these groups, you just need to subtract the round number and leave the remaining digits as 32nds. For instance, let's say the number you want to translate is 3212. You know that 3200 equals 100. Hence, 3212 translates into 100-12. If the number is 3192, you know that 3168 is equal to 99-00. So you subtract 3168 from 3192 and you have the answer: 99-24.

7

The Five-Day LSS Oscillator: How to Measure Market Strength

There are many ways to measure market strength. This is just one method that takes into account the previous five trading days. Sophisticated traders will want to smooth the oscillator numbers over a period of three readings. Yet the reading itself is helpful in that it can be used to gauge mildly bullish or bearish market conditions or more extreme overbought or oversold markets.

Question

Using the following set of numbers, generate the LSS five-day oscillator number. Does this number suggest that the current market is bullish or bearish?

Day	Open	High	Low	Close
1	1175.50	1180.40	1151.00	1154.90
2	1144.00	1185.40	1144.00	1172.40
3	1157.50	1161.30	1127.20	1127.30
4	1141.80	1146.00	1129.60	1130.70
5	1131.00	1153.50	1117.30	1128.80

Answer

The place to start is with the formula for the oscillator:

Highest price in last 5 days – Open 5 days ago = X

Last close – Lowest price in last 5 days = Y

$$\frac{(X + Y) \times 100}{(\text{Highest price in last 5 days} - \text{Lowest price in last 5 days}) \times 2}$$

Highest price in last 5 days = 1185.40

Open 5 days ago = 1175.50

Therefore, 1185.40 (highest price) – 1175.50 (open 5 days ago) = 9.90 = X

Last close = 1128.80

Lowest price in last 5 days = 1117.30

Therefore, 1128.80 (last close) − 1117.30 (lowest price) =
11.50 = Y

$$\frac{(9.90 \ [X] + 11.50 \ [Y])}{(1185.40 \ [\text{highest price}] - 1117.30 \ [\text{lowest price}])}$$

$$= \frac{2140}{68.1}$$

= 34.6 percent = LSS five-day oscillator value

This reading suggests that the market is currently bearish.

8

The 3-Day Difference: How to Measure Market Momentum

The rate at which a market rises or falls can be an important indicator that a top or bottom is near. As a market soars higher, the rate of its rise will slow as it nears the top; conversely, when a market breaks, the time will come when it is still falling, but at a slower rate than when the descent first began.

Question

Using the following oscillator numbers, determine whether the market is bullish or bearish and whether the rate at which the market is rising or declining is increasing or decreasing.

Day	Oscillator Value	3-Day Difference
1	77.4%	—
2	88.6%	—
3	52.8%	—
4	67.5%	−9.9
5	49.3%	−39.3
6	37.5%	−15.3
7	52.4%	−15.1
8	77.0%	+27.7

Answer

In this example, the bottom day was either Day 6 or 7 when the 3-day difference was still negative, but less negative than Day 5. By Day 8, the market had clearly turned the corner, given the high oscillator reading. As the negative numbers become more negative (see Day 5), the market gains negative momentum. No market can continue lower, however, without bargain-hunters and profit-takers entering. This tends to slow the rate of negative momentum, and the market gains strength. These numbers suggest that there was a good buying opportunity on Day 6 or 7. By Day 8, there may have been good opportunities to buy early in the day near the lows. Later, the market staged a strong rally.

9

Chart Patterns: Finding Symmetry in the Market

Chart patterns tend to mirror one another. This is the symmetry that exists in so many markets. If a market rises in the morning, it may give back all its gains during the afternoon. If a market breaks in the morning, it may regain the entire lost ground by day's end. Sometimes rising morning patterns are mirrored by afternoon rising patterns—the classic trend day up. Likewise, weak mornings can be reflected by weak afternoons. What's so amazing about these patterns is how symmetrical they are.

Question

Where is this market going?

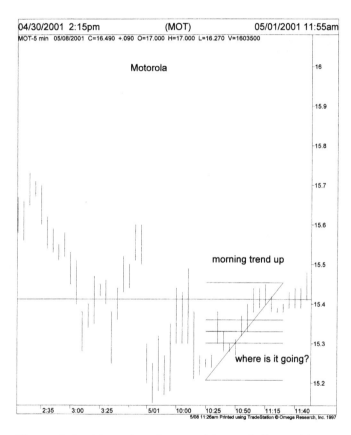

Figure 9.1   Note that the trend is up, followed by a consolidation phase.

Answer

Wasn't it obvious? You can view the morning trend as the first leg of a trend that will be mirrored in the afternoon. Note that even if an upward move is followed by a downward move, the pattern is still symmetrical.

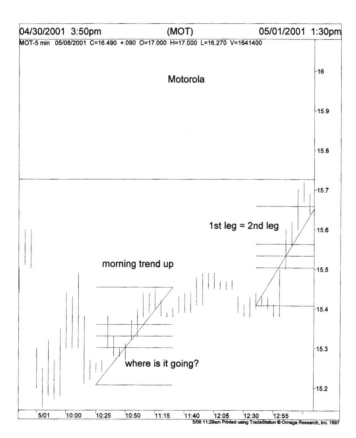

Figure 9.2 Following the noon-hour consolidation, a second uptrend leg is formed.

10

Price Reversals: When the Symmetry "Fails"

One of the advantages of time and price trading is having a pulse on the market. You know what to expect in terms of market action for both time and price. When the symmetry fails, however, you have to reevaluate your position. Typically, a failure swing suggests a price reversal. This offers the classic opportunity to get out and reverse.

Question

Can you see the failure swing in the chart below?

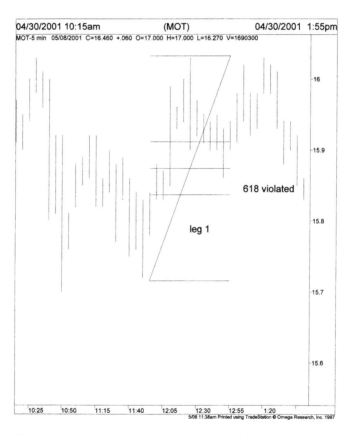

Figure 10.1   Note the penetration of the .618
retracement line.

Answer

Notice what happened following the failure swing. When the market does not behave as anticipated, chances are a reversal is in the offing.

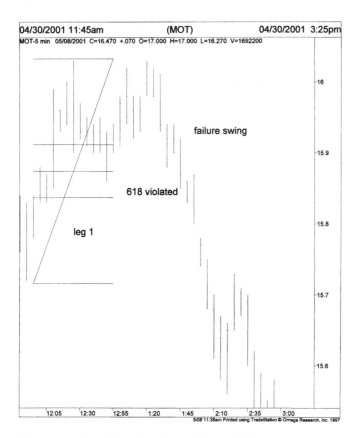

Figure 10.2 The violation of the .618 retracement suggests a failure swing.

11

Thursdays: The Weakest (Strongest) Day of the Week

We've researched over 577 Thursdays in our day-of-the-week studies. Our composite charts reveal an interesting Thursday phenomenon. But you must know what kind of market you are trading.

Questions

In what kind of a market do you want to be an aggressive seller on
Thursday?

In what kind of a market do you want to be an aggressive buyer on
Thursday?

What is the ideal pattern leading up to a Thursday when you want
to sell?

What is the ideal pattern leading up to a Thursday when you want
to buy?

Answers

Thursdays tend to be the weakest day of the week in bull markets. During bear markets, Thursdays tend to rally as the countertrend day.

The idea pattern for selling on Thursday is following two or
three days of rising prices—the classic 3-day pattern. The ideal
pattern for buying on Thursday is following two or three days of
falling prices.

12

Stops: Where to Pull the Plug

Many traders think you should place your stop based on how much money you are willing to lose. This is a mistake. Stop placement is an art form. A stop must not be placed too close to the current market price. A distant stop creates other problems.

Questions

Where's the one place you must never place a stop?

When trailing a stop, what's the one thing you don't want to do?

What's the maximum percentage distance you want to let the
   market retrace, prior to a resumption of positive prices?

How do you detect stop-running?

What's the relationship of stop placement to volatility?

Answers

Just above prior highs or just below prior lows is a dangerous
place for stops. This is because many stops are often jammed
together at these prices, inviting stop-runners to raid the stops.
Prior intraday highs and lows are also areas where stops will accu-
mulate.

When trailing a stop, you must move the stop in a positive
direction only. If the market is moving higher and you are long,
your trailing sell stop must be moved higher. Conversely, if you are
short and the market is moving lower, you must move your buy
stop down—never higher—as the position gains profits.

The maximum amount you want the market to retrace is .618 of
the initial move. You don't want the stop placed exactly at the .618
point, but slightly below or above that level, depending upon
whether you are buying or selling. The reason is, stop-runners will
often target the stops at that level. Once the market has retraced
more than .618, chances are the market is going to continue to
trend in its current direction.

Stop-running is characterized by what is known as *price rejection.* The market swiftly moves lower, only to stage a sudden

recovery. At highs, the market will often surge up on short-covering, go dead at the top, and quickly move lower. Once the stops are run, the market usually moves in the opposite direction.

As market volatility increases, the stops must be moved further away from the current market price. This only makes sense, because otherwise random moves will cause the stops to be hit. Try to avoid placing your stop where other traders have placed theirs. An abundance of stops at one price will trigger panic buying or selling and you will receive a bad fill as a result.

13

Mondays: The Ideal Day to Buy

Our research demonstrates that if you had one day to buy, Monday would be that ideal day if bullish conditions prevail. There are also accompanying factors that you want to take into account as a Monday buyer.

Question

What's the ideal pattern for a Monday buying opportunity?

Answer

Not all Mondays offer excellent buying opportunities, so you must be careful when looking to buy on a Monday. First, it helps if you are already in a bull market. This is not hard to determine. Second, you want the recent market action, as measured by the one- and five-day strength index, to be strong, with a percentage over 50. Third, you want the market to demonstrate strength at the close of trading on the prior trading day, usually a Friday. If the prior day closes on or near the low, chances are the market will continue lower on Monday instead of moving higher. The one-day strength index will provide you a good reading on how bullish the market was on the prior day. Last, you want a steady-to-higher open to occur on the Monday buying day. A sharply higher or sharply lower open on Monday presents real problems. With a sharply higher open, the market may spend the rest of the day trading down to more reasonable levels. With a sharply lower open, the market may continue to sell off the rest of the day. A higher open is always good for buyers.

14

Time and Price Trading: How to Target the Exit Level and the Point of Maximum Adversity

---

With time and price trading, the parameters of the trade are spelled out, once you know important key information—namely, the direction of the move, the size of the first leg, the subsequent equilibrium point, and, significantly, the length of time of the trend. Armed with this information, you are ready to map out a winning trading strategy.

Question

Given the following information, determine where the market is going, when it is going to get there, your profit point, and where you would place your stop.

Direction of first leg: Up

High of first leg: 1188.00

Low of first leg: 1181.00

Minutes to create first leg: 11

Equilibrium point: 1187.00

Answer

The range on the first leg is 7.00 points (1188.00 − 1181.00), so you are looking for a 7.00-point rally on the second leg. The market should rally this amount off the 1187.00 equilibrium point, making 1194.00 the target sell price. You will try to buy the market at or near the *equilibrium price.* Once you have purchased the market, you need to have a stop-loss order in case you are wrong. This stop-loss should be placed slightly below 1183.70. To arrive at this stop-loss number, you need to take the range of the first leg (7.00) and multiply it by .618. You then *subtract* this amount from the high of the first leg. [Note: If the market were breaking, you would *add* this amount to the low of the first leg.] Here's how these numbers were generated:

$$7.00 \text{ (first-leg range)} \times .618 = 4.30$$

$$1188.00 \text{ (first-leg high)} - 4.30 \text{ (.618 of range)} = 1183.70$$

This represents the point of *maximum adversity*. This is the amount that the market can move lower and still be good to the upside. Do not confuse this with thinking that the market must move down by this amount. In a truly bullish environment this will rarely be the case. Rather, this is the maximum adversity you will take on the position.

Next, you want to deal with the element of *time*. If the symmetry is to prevail, the second leg will have an 11-minute rally (move in one direction). You cannot pinpoint the exact minute without knowing when the rally begins. This could occur within ten minutes of the establishment of the equilibrium price, or as long as 45 minutes to an hour after it's first established. However, once the rally begins to break out above the prior high of 1188.00, you know the move is under way. Look for the *lowest price* of that rally and call that one-minute bar "minute one." You then count forward until you reach the eleventh minute going forward, and that should be the top bar—hopefully, near or at the target sell price.

The patterns do not always fulfill themselves in both time and price. The top bar may occur on the eleventh minute into the rally, but a number of points below the target price. Or, perhaps, you might reach the target sell price before the pattern becomes fulfilled in time. In either case, take the profit and move on to the next trade.

15

Confirming Indicators: Divergence Tools That Pinpoint Price Reversals

A number of confirming indicators demonstrate whether the market is headed higher or lower. In most instances, these indicators can be used to quickly judge whether you are on the right side of the market. At other times, one or more of the indicators may serve as divergence tools, moving in the *opposite* direction of the price trend. When this occurs, the market is often poised to reverse.

Question

Name five or more leading indicators for stock index futures.

Answer

Premium, cash, Dow Jones Averages, TICK, TICKI.

Question

In the following chart, can you spot the divergence between the price and leading indicator?

Answer

Figure 15.1 Notice the divergence between prices and the leading indicator.

16

Yesterday's Close: How to Use the 1-Day Strength Indicator to Measure Strength

Where the market closed yesterday is vitally important to how it will trade today. Typically, a strong close will suggest higher prices today, and a weak close will suggest lower prices today. For this reason, we want to translate yesterday's close into a strength percentage.

Question

Given the following set of prices for the day just completed, calculate the one-day strength percentage for tomorrow.

High = 1268.30

Low = 1240.20

Close = 1257.20

Answer

Since 0 (zero) percentage represents a close at the low, and 100 percentage represents a close at the high, a close in midrange should be in the 50 percent area.

Here's the formula for calculating the one-day strength:

$$\frac{(\text{Close} - \text{Low})}{(\text{High} - \text{Low})} = \text{one-day strength percentage}$$

$$\frac{(1257.20 - 1240.20)}{(1268.30 - 1240.20)} = \frac{1700}{28.10}$$

$$= 60.50\% \text{ one-day strength percentage}$$

This particular reading suggests a slightly bullish condition at the close of yesterday's market.

17

Gap Trades: When to Fade the Opening

Market openings present trading opportunities that are often over-looked by many traders. When an opening price exceeds the prior day's high or, under some circumstances, the prior day's closing-bar high, a so-called *gap* will appear on the charts. The same is true when the opening price falls below either the prior day's low or the prior day's closing bar.

Questions

What's the best way to trade an opening gap to the upside or downside? What's the probability that the gap will be *filled* at some time during the trading day?

Answer

Opening gaps to the upside should be sold; opening gaps to the downside should be bought. The percentages favor the filling of a gap approximately 75 percent of the time. So-called *extreme* gaps—when prices open far away from the prior day's closing price—should not be *faded,* since such extreme moves suggest continued movement in the direction of the gap.

18

Self-Assessment: Can You Learn from Mistakes?

Anyone can memorize formulas and learn mechanical rules, but can you learn from your mistakes? The real transformation from novice to professional trader comes from internalizing lessons learned. If you have ever made a mistake in the market and paid dearly, an opportunity has presented itself to you. Can you learn the lesson of that loss? Did it help you challenge an assumption or preconception or belief? People who cannot learn from the past are doomed to repeat their failures. Are you a person who can learn from past mistakes?

Questions

Are you ever deceived by your opinions? Are your opinions truly your own, or do you rely on the advice of others? Are you an independent thinker? What was the last important lesson that you learned in the market? What did it cost you? If you know anyone who has been successful in the market, how do they cope with market adversity? Do they take losses in stride? Or are they devastated by losses?

Good judgment comes from experience. If life were a series of effortless exercises, few of us would have the character to withstand adversity. Consider the following statements:

- I am willing to acknowledge mistakes.

- I learn from my mistakes and rarely make the same mistake twice.

- I tend to question authority.

- I persevere in the face of obstacles.

- I look upon adversity as a minor setback, an opportunity to grow.

Answers

There are no right or wrong answers here. An hour spent thinking about what motivates you in the market is well worth whatever effort it takes.

You need to be rigorous with yourself. Do you repeatedly become stubborn in the face of market adversity and refuse to accept the inevitable, resulting in large losses? Perhaps you need to think about what you are doing. Is refusing to take a loss an ego thing with you? Are you trying to prove yourself right by proving the market wrong? There are many ways to self-destruct in the market and this is one of them. You need to spend some time thinking about what motivates you on an unconscious basis. Sometimes you can try and try and try before an answer appears. The best answers are rarely easily won. You have to expend effort to find what works for you and what doesn't.

For most people, I suspect you'll find a pattern. You always give up right before the big success, or you cannot leave a good thing alone. You take small profits when large profits are there for the person with patience. The greatest sense of accomplishment occurs when you can correctly identify one of the mistakes you are repeating—and then stop doing it.

19

Finding the Two Major Daily Trends: The Best Times to Trade Every Day

There are two major daily trends per day. Due to changes in volatility and the differences among markets, it is impossible to put a point value on what constitutes a major trend. But if you study daily chart patterns, you will begin to see when these trends appear.

Question

When do the two major trends occur?

Answer

In most markets, you will see two daily patterns occur, one in the morning and one in the afternoon. When the morning trend fails to occur before 12 noon East Coast time, the trend will typically occur during the noon hour. Because of the symmetry in the market, you often have trends which are of similar point value, though not always in the same direction.

20

Pit Traders: The Basics

Every trader needs to understand the basics of how orders are executed on the floor of a futures exchange. First and foremost, a trader needs to understand that there are a buyer and seller involved in every trade. Moreover, every trade is consummated in a trading pit. The sole exception to this is when you trade a contract such as the E-mini. There is no centralized trading pit for this contract. In recent years, this form of on-line trading has become increasingly popular.

Questions

When I place an order with my broker at the XYZ brokerage house, how is it executed? How is the price established? What kind of orders can I place?

Answers

All orders are transmitted to the floor of the appropriate futures exchange where the contract is traded. If you are trading a metal such as silver or copper, your order will be sent to the futures exchange in New York. If you are trading grains or meats, your order will be sent to the Chicago Board of Trade or the Chicago Mercantile Exchange. Once the order arrives at the desk of the firm that your broker is using to clear its trades, the order is sent into the trading pit via runner or hand signal. The order is then given to an order-filling broker who bids or offers the order, depending on whether you want to buy or sell. The job of the broker is to get you the best possible price as soon as possible given the restrictions you have placed on the order. If you place a *market* order, the broker will often just *hit* the offer if you are buying, or hit the bid if you are selling. For a trade to be consummated, both buyer and seller have to agree on a single price. If you place a *limit* order, you place a limit on how high you will buy or how low you will sell. Let's say the Treasury bonds are trading at 102-13. You want to buy them, but you only want to pay 102-10, which is below the market. So you place a limit order to buy bonds at 102-10 on a limit. The broker understands that you are willing to pay less—called *or better*—but not more. Now he must find a seller willing to sell at that price. Since a *bid,* or buying price, will exist, there will likewise be an *offer,* or selling price. The bid is the highest price the buyers are willing to pay, and the offer is the lowest price at which the sellers are willing to sell. The difference between the two is known as the *spread.* The spread can be one or more ticks, depending upon the liquidity and volatility of the market. All the trades are consummated in the pit via what is known as *open outcry*. That means that bids and offers are yelled out, and willing traders must agree on a single price for a trade to take place. This open outcry system gives everyone a chance to participate in the trading, and it prevents private deals from taking place away from the prevailing market price.

There are other orders you can place. You can place *stop* orders that become market orders once a given price is reached. You can place MOC (market on close) orders, which must take place in the final minute of trading. There are also *market on open* (MOO) orders, which, understandably, are consummated on the opening of trading. You can place *fill-or-kill* orders that are limit orders; these must be executed immediately or not at all. MIT (market if touched) orders work like stop orders.

Once an order is filled in the pit, it is transmitted back to your broker, reversing the process. The fill may be hand-signaled to the clearing firm's desk, or a runner may take the physical piece of paper and carry it back to the desk. In either instance, the information to known to all parties right away. Meanwhile, on the floor, the buyer and seller of your trade *card* the information: futures, contract month, quantity, price and initials of the opposing broker. This information is then entered into a centralized computer and sent to the clearinghouse that is a party to all trades. The floor broker also makes a note of your clearing firm so that you are properly credited for having taken the trade. This is a remarkably efficient system that has worked, with few problems, for over 150 years.

21

The Five-Day Average Range: Measuring the Market's Volatility

A simple calculation, the five-day range has a variety of uses. You can superimpose the five-day average range over an early high or low and extrapolate a possible market bottom or top. When compared with the range of the day just completed, the five-day range provides a yardstick against which to measure the likelihood of tomorrow's range falling within its parameters. Should you wish to take a trade late in the day, the average range can often tell you what's left in the market.

Question

Taking the prices shown below, calculate the five-day average range:

Day	High	Low
1	1137.20	1123.50
2	1140.30	1124.00
3	1166.70	1141.80
4	1189.80	1166.60
5	1215.00	1193.90

Answer

The formula for calculating the five-day range is to take each daily range (high – low), sum the five ranges, and divide by five. Accordingly, the calculations are as follows:

Day	Range
1	13.70
2	16.30
3	24.90
4	23.20
5	21.10

When you add these range numbers together, the sum is 99.20. Divided by five, the five-day average range is 19.80 points.

On Day 6, let's assume you have an early high of 1230.00 and an early low of 1219.00, eleven points difference. Assuming that one of these numbers will hold through the close of trading and that the day's volatility will at least equal the five-day average, you can then calculate the anticipated high and low. The anticipated low would be 1210.20 (1230.00 early high − 19.80 average range = 1210.20), and the anticipated high would be 1238.80 (1219.00 early high + 19.80 average range = 1238.80). It is unlikely that both numbers will be hit, but the probabilities do favor one of the numbers being hit.

The five-day average range can also be used as a guideline of what to expect on the following day. With average range close to 20 points, don't expect a 13-point range; on the other hand, the market is unlikely to move 30 points, although exceptions are always possible.

Because the LSS pivotal buy and sell numbers are generated on the prior day's range, you must be careful in using these numbers when the prior day's range is very high or very low, relative to the average range. A low-volatility prior day will generate entries close to the market, and you may get in prematurely on a random move higher or lower. A high-volatility prior day will generate entries too far away from the market. Hence, you may find yourself buying the top or selling the bottom.

22

Stock Market Seasonal Trends: The Best Time to Buy and Sell

Despite the absence of growing and harvesting seasons, the stock market demonstrates some of the most consistent and reliable seasonal trends. It pays to know the most prominent seasonal trends, since this knowledge can prevent you from becoming too bullish at a seasonal peak or too bearish at a seasonal low.

Question

Name the most basic seasonal trends in the stock market for the following periods of the year: January, late March or early April, July or August, October, and the trend into the end of the year.

Answer

In a nutshell, the general trends favor a decline in early January (perhaps profit-taking selling), followed by a mid-January rally. By late March or early April the market often reaches a peak, followed by a choppy market in mid-April, perhaps related to the April 15 tax deadline. The early summer months are often characterized by a midsummer rally, culminating in a market top in late July or early August. September and October are typically down months in the stock market (witness the 1929 Crash and the 1987 October decline), with the lows occurring sometime in late October (a good buying opportunity?). The trend into the end of the year is typically bullish, with the first two weeks in December characterized by a robust market. The Christmas holidays are typically quiet, with choppy and thin markets.

There are always exceptions to these genuine trends, but the overall pattern is remarkably consistent.

23

Learning to "Embrace the Uncertainty": Finding Profits on the First Trade

---

It is only human nature to want certainty. Yet this very desire often puts us at a disadvantage in the market. By seeking a sure-thing, we typically are late in getting in the market, and late in taking profits when getting out. Is there a better time to enter or exit the market? And, if so, how do we know for certain that we are right?

Question

You've just witnessed the most amazing confirmation of your trading methodology. The market just completed a four-day winning streak of your buy and sell signals, but you were only trading on paper. Tomorrow you want to back up your opinion with real money. Should you?

Answer

No matter how brilliant your trading strategies, winning streaks—like losing streaks—tend to repeat in cycles. Assuming your trading methodology wins profits over time, you are better off waiting until you sustain several days of losses than jumping in at the top of the equity curve. Even the best systems have periods of losses. To expect a winning cycle to occur unabated is a big mistake. Chances favor a winning trade coming off a series of losing days—*if* you have a winning strategy.

24

Price Rejection: What It Means

Price rejection usually manifests itself at daily or intraday highs and lows. Price rejection usually occurs quickly, since the market spends very little time at daily highs or lows. Once rejected, prices often retreat back to the middle.

Question

Can you identify the point of price rejection on the chart in Figure 24.1?

Figure 24.1   When prices are rejected at a prior high or low, it almost always signals a price reversal.

Answer

Notice how the market reverses direction once the stops have been run. When prices go to new lows or new highs, they should continue in the direction of the breakout. When this does not occur, it means prices will reverse.

25

Strategies for Getting out of Trouble: Exit-and-Reverse and Averaging

Not every trading strategy works as one would like. Sometimes, you simply pick the wrong side of the market; at other times, your buying or selling is premature. These two strategies are designed to undo the damage and get you back on the road to profits. They are aggressive strategies, however, and require specific market conditions to work.

Question

What are the market conditions that best lend themselves to utilizing the exit-and-reverse strategy and the averaging strategy?

Answer

The two are decidedly different and used under different circumstances. The *exit-and-reverse strategy* is used when you are fairly certain you are on the wrong side of the market, *and* the market is about to run in the opposite direction. First, you take the loss on the initial position. Second, you immediately reverse direction by taking the opposite position. This strategy can be accomplished with one order, but you usually want to think of the strategy as two distinct transactions. An aggressive variation of this strategy is to double the number of contracts when you reverse. This means if you lose ten ticks on one contract, you need only five ticks on two contracts in order to break even.

You can also implement this strategy as one transaction. Let's say you are bearish on the market. You sell one contract in anticipation of lower prices. As soon as you sell, though, the market moves higher, creating a loss on the position. Fearing the market is about to shoot higher, you immediately reverse by buying three contracts. One contract offsets the loss in the short position. The other two make you net long two contracts. Now you only need one-half the move in the second two-lot position to offset the entire loss in the first single-lot position. For this strategy to work, it must be implemented quickly, as soon as you sense that your initial position is wrong. Should you wait too long, the move in the opposite direction may have already occurred. You also risk getting *whipsawed* in the position, in which case you will lose on both positions. This strategy is best utilized, therefore, shortly after the open or just before a significant trend is about to occur. A conservative exit-and-reverse strategy is to use this technique only to recoup losses. Once you are even, you exit the second position and begin rethinking your next trade.

The *averaging strategy* is used in an entirely different market environment. You use this strategy when you may have entered the market prematurely but when the position still looks good. When selling, you sell more as the market rises against you; when buying, you buy more as the market declines against you. Most traders are reluctant to try this because they are following the rule that you never average a loss. Under most circumstances, this makes sense. When the market is consolidating, however, it is appropriate to buy or sell more, as long as it doesn't break out from that area. This means you must know where the support and resistance levels are. The advantage of averaging is that you get a higher sell price and a lower buy price. Moreover, you have taken on additional contracts; hence, any gains will be magnified. When you average, you must keep a tight rein on your position. You probably don't want to average more than three times, and you want the final position to be profitable immediately. If it is not, exit the entire position immediately! In time and price trading, you can average within the buy zone, from the equilibrium down to the .618 pullback. When selling, sell within the sell zone, from the equilibrium up to the .618 pullback. Beyond the .618, you must run, lest you end up with serious losses.

26

The Relationship of Yesterday's Close to Today's Open: Where Should You Buy? Where Should You Sell?

There is an important relationship between yesterday's close and today's open. If the market is going higher, does it make much difference where you buy? How about selling in a declining market? You could make the case that bottom-line profits are the only important criteria for a winning strategy. There are patterns that demonstrate the best opportunities for buying and selling, and those are the ones we will examine here.

Questions

How do you want the market to open if you are buying today? How do you want the market to open if you are selling? What is the key relationship between yesterday's close and today's open?

Answers

There is a paradox at work here. Buying strategies do better when the market opens higher. Selling strategies do better when the market opens lower. Doesn't this contradict the notion of buying low and selling high? No. When you buy above yesterday's close, the probabilities favor the position. The same is true when you sell below yesterday's close. You don't want to buy too high above yesterday's close and you don't want to sell too low below yesterday's close. On the contrary, you want the market to open slightly higher when buying, and slightly lower when selling.

One way to look at the relationship between the prior day's close and today's open is in terms of the average daily range. If the average daily range is 20.00 points, and the market opens 7.00 higher, chances are you have another 13.00 points to the upside. But if the average daily range is 20.00 points and the market opens 14.00 points higher, you may be looking at only 6.00 points to the top. Chances are, in this scenario, the large gap up on the opening will be filled and the market will trade lower. The same notion, in reverse, applies to selling on the open. If a market opens too low, bargain-hunters may bid the market up, closing the gap. The paradox is that slightly lower is a good sell, but lower still may offer a buying opportunity. If the market opens extremely lower, however, you want to be a seller, since the bottom may be falling out. So much of what works is a matter of degree. It is difficult to have one blanket rule that covers all situations.

27

Market Sentiment:
Another Timing Tool

If you can remember the bullish enthusiasm for purchasing stocks during March 2000, right at the market top, you will understand this concept. The market is always the most bullish at the top and the most bearish at the bottom. This notion of trading against market sentiment is known as *contrary opinion,* and it almost always generates substantial profits for those willing to bet against the crowd.

Questions

What does contrary opinion measure? How can you use it to pin-point turning points in the market?

Answers

Contrary opinion attempts to measure market sentiment, specifically, the degree of bullishness or bearishness among traders at a given time. There are companies that specialize in generating market sentiment numbers on a daily and weekly basis. The numbers are published in *Barron's* and other periodicals. Another source is "Market Vane's" Bullish Consensus percentages that are available to subscribers via e-mail on a daily basis. Typically, the higher the percentage reading, the more bullish the market. If the Bullish Consensus percentage is just 12 percent, you have a very bearish sentiment; a reading of 97 percent would be extremely bullish. The key to using the numbers is to *fade*—or trade against—extreme readings. Hence, a market that has a 94 percent bullish sentiment is ripe for a selloff and should be sold, because everybody has already done their buying at that stage. They are waiting for new buyers to enter the market and push prices higher. At the first sign of weakness, the buyers will all rush to the exits at once, offering the market lower. This, in turn, will generate additional selling and soon you will be off to the races—lower. This phenomenon works in reverse at a market bottom. Gloom and doom will prevail when prices have fallen to their lows. This will be reflected by a low market sentiment, typically 10 percent or lower. Such a market is ripe for reversal.

There are other ways to use market sentiment, but its most significant value comes as a reversal signal in overbought or oversold markets. One disadvantage with interpreting the numbers comes at the market extremes. A market might be 80 percent bullish but still rising. How do you know you aren't selling prematurely when you sell such a market? The reading can get high and stay high. For this reason, you probably want to consult other reversal indicators when planning to pick a top or a bottom.

28

Tuesdays: The Afternoon Opportunity

Our 12-year study of day-of-the-week patterns reveals a hidden opportunity on Tuesday afternoons. Following on the heels of a strong Monday, Tuesday mornings tend to be a lackadaisical affair. But, by mid-afternoon, a genuine opportunity seems to occur with sufficient regularity to warrant a market signal.

Questions

What is the prevalent market pattern that occurs on Tuesday afternoon? When does it occur?

Answers

The composite chart for S&P futures clearly demonstrates a buying opportunity for Tuesday afternoons. The typical rally occurs at approximately 2:30 P.M. East Coast time.

29

Market Engineering: How the Market Stages a Rally— and a Decline

George Douglas Taylor first observed this phenomenon in the grain markets in the 1950s. He claimed the market was "engineered from within" to repeat a three-day cycle that consisted of a buy day, a sell day, and a short sell day, hence my designation of LSS to mean *long, sell,* and *sell short.* In observing a variety of markets since Taylor first made this observation, it appears that very little has changed. The same patterns appear routinely in the futures, options, and equity markets.

Question

What is market engineering and how does it manifest itself in the market?

Answer

Human nature today is very much as it was fifty or even a hundred years ago. People don't like to lose money and they can be intimidated into acting against their own interests by inducing the element of fear. Likewise, the greed side of the equation hasn't changed, either. One is likely to let down his guard if he thinks the profits will continue to flow. This is the central premise of Taylor's theory of market engineering.

On the so-called buy day, Taylor claimed that knowledgeable market forces sold the market down in order to create a buying opportunity for themselves. Strong hands, according to Taylor, caused the market to decline. The ensuing losses then caused the weak hands to abandon positions and sell out their positions—to, naturally, the strong hands. In the market, these transactions were manifested by a decline followed by a strong rally.

On the second day of the three-day cycle, the strong hands would often take profits at, through, slightly above, or below the previous day's high. By the third day, the market engineering was back in full force. Now the strong hands wanted a selling opportunity, so they created a rally to cause the weak hands to want to jump aboard lest they miss a spectacular opportunity. The weak hands jump in as buyers, and the strong hands sell at the artificial highs. Once the market fails to rally off the highs, the weak hands throw in the towel and sell out their positions at a loss—to, of course, the strong hands, the same people who are now covering their short-sale positions and earning big profits. If you don't think the rich get richer in the market, you better think again.

I cannot find anything illegal about this activity since everyone seems to be operating in his or her own self-interest in the market. On the buy day, the sellers at the bottom are selling because they are fearful the market will break lower. That's the fear component. On the short-sale day buying at the top, the buyers want to get aboard a good thing, albeit three days late, lest they miss an excellent rally. That's the greed component. In a sense, everyone gets what he or she wants. Unfortunately, only those who buy low and sell high can earn the profits.

Looked at another way, the market goes down to go up—and vice versa.

30

The Psychological Component: How to Avoid the Most Common Pitfalls

Most people are caught between the proverbial rock and a hard place when it comes to trading. Either their fear of losing keeps them from picking up the phone and taking a trade, or their recklessness causes them to overtrade, in which case they cannot put the phone down.

The ideal is a middle course. The fearful trader needs to reevaluate his reasons for being in the market. Can he endure the risks of day-to-day trading, or must he have certainty before he enters a trade? The reckless trader might view the market the way a teenager sees a video game—perhaps a fun way to pass the time. The trader enjoys the rush, the thrills of trading. But can he make any money?

Questions

You mapped out your strategy last night. You knew you wanted to buy the market at a specific price today. When the market reached that price, however, you said, "Wait a minute. It looks like it might trade lower. Let's watch it for a while." Needless to say, that was the bottom. The market surged higher and you weren't aboard. What held you back from executing your game plan?

Or consider this scenario. You've been making reckless and uninformed trades lately and your equity is down. You need to score big today to make up for those reckless losses. So you double the number of contracts on a market order. At first, the market goes your way. You are feeling good. But then adversity hits, and you decide you won't give up without a fight. At first, you begin to get some of your profits back. But then disaster hits. You sustain the biggest loss of your trading career. How do you react?

Answers

In both instances, the answer is the same: Stop trading. At least for the moment. You are not in a psychological frame of mind that permits dispassionate self-analysis. After the dust settles, you need to go back and reevaluate what you are doing. The fearful trader needs to learn to step up to the plate. The reckless trader needs to learn discipline. Both can be mastered if you are determined to succeed.

If you see yourself here, you are not alone. The psychological aspects of trading are among the hardest to master. It is one thing to know what to do and quite another to do it. Until you can wed your market knowledge with your psychological knowledge, you are going to be at a disadvantage in the market. Never mind that most people face the same pitfalls. This is a little like saying that misery loves company. The challenge is to rise above, and overcome, your shortcomings.

The place to start is with a rigorous self-analysis or with help from a competent professional who understands how self-destructive instincts can hold an individual back. You really have to have it out with yourself. Since everyone is different, it is hard to suggest a single, easy solution. But let's say you are clearly fearful of losing money, and that is what is holding you back from picking up the phone. Ask yourself this: If I don't pick up the phone and take the trade, what is going to happen? The answer is you are going to create a whole sort of other problems. For instance:

1. I won't have the profits, or perhaps losses.

2. I may decide to *chase* the trade, in which case the profits may be smaller, or the risk higher.

3. I will beat myself up for missing a good opportunity.

4. My account will suffer because I will need those profits that I missed to offset the inevitable losses of trading.

5. I will repeat the same mistake next time.

6. I will think I'm no good at trading.

7. I will attribute the other person's good fortune to simply having good luck.

I think you can see where I'm going with this. First and foremost, you need to decide the most basic question: Do you want to continue trading? If the answer is a resounding "yes!" then you need to resolve to do what you fear most, then continue doing it until you are comfortable. If this means you are determined to take tomorrow's trade regardless of the outcome, then you have to set your emotions aside and take the trade exactly as you planned the very next day. Then you need to repeat this pattern again on the second day, and so on. By doing this, you will be training yourself to overcome your fear—which, I understand, can be a formidable obstacle to success in the market. There can be only two outcomes to your decision to do this. You will sustain losses because your trading strategies are faulty. This means back to the trading boards. Or you will begin to earn profits and have confidence in what you are doing. If you try and fail, you will have learned a valuable lesson. Perhaps the market isn't for you. You can move on to something else. There's no failure in trying.

The outcome for the trader who lacks discipline should likewise prove valuable. By putting down the phone and concentrating on the best opportunities, you will be allowing yourself to succeed. Your account will start to grow, and that should compensate you for any loss of thrills that you used to gain from trading. Having discipline in your life creates an inner confidence that is hard to duplicate in practically any other endeavor. Trading is a little bit like drinking. Having a predinner cocktail can be highly stimulating and enjoyable, but guzzling a whole bottle will create problems in your life like you wouldn't believe. Think about where you want to go and try to find a path that will take you there. The best traders are disciplined traders.

31

The Weekly Stock Market Pattern: How the Market Trades

While not every week will trade in this pattern, there is ample evidence that the market has a reliable price pattern. In stronger markets, the rallies will be stronger and the breaks weaker. In weaker markets, the rallies will be weaker and the breaks stronger.

Question

What is the typical weekly pattern for stock prices as reflected in the major averages and indices?

Answer

Given that a variety of factors will determine how any one-day price pattern will appear, there is a consistent pattern that appears:

1. *Monday* tends to be the strongest day of the week with upward price pressure beginning at the open. This is particularly true if the averages closed in the upper range of the day's range on the prior trading day.

2. *Tuesday* tends to consolidate in the morning hours with additional upward pressure on prices in the afternoon.

3. *Wednesday* tends to be the choppiest day of the week. In general, though, bullish markets will see prices closing near the highs on Wednesday, whereas bearish markets tend to close near the lows on Wednesday.

4. *Thursday* is the countertrend day. If the market has been up on the prior three days, look for selling to push prices lower on Thursday. The exception is when you are in a bear market and the prior three days have been lower. In this instance, Thursday typically will rally.

5. *Friday* tends to open strong and rally temporarily. Initial selling will often push the market lower on Friday morning following a higher open. By early afternoon, bargain hunters, in anticipation of Monday's price boost, will bid up prices into the close.

32

Your First Trade:
How to Place an Order

Often the easiest things about trading create the most questions.
How does a new trader go about placing an order? In the current
world of discount brokerage, there is less hands-on help in the
form of helpful brokers and more anonymous order takers on the
other end of the line. Because mistakes can prove costly, it is
absolutely vital that you place your order with precision. Moreover, because timing is so important, you must be able to give the
order both accurately and quickly.

Question

You see an opportunity to make money in the U.S. Treasury bond futures by purchasing bonds in anticipation of rumors of an impending interest rate cut by the Fed. With the nearby September Treasury bond contract trading at 101-03, you decide to place a limit order to buy two September bond futures contracts at 101-00. You also know that once you are in the position, you want to place a stop-loss order six ticks ($187.50 per contract) below your entry price. Assuming the order is filled and the stop is not, you plan to take profits one basis point higher, at 102-00. What do you tell your broker?

Answer

We are talking about three separate orders here: a limit entry order, a stop order (if you are filled), and, assuming the order is filled and the stop not hit, an exit order. To the person taking your order, an order is an order, so you want to treat each order separately. Even before you call the broker, you want to write down the order. Once you call, the broker will read back the order and ask you if you are in agreement with him. Here's what you write down:

"Buy two September bond futures 101-00."

Here's what you tell your broker when he picks up the phone:

"This is John Jones. For Account No. 23848, I want to buy two September bond futures at 101 even, or better, day only."

He will repeat what you just said and ask for your confirmation. Once you agree, he will typically assign this order with a ticket number so that it can be tracked, saying:

"For account No. 23848, you want to buy two September bond futures at 101 even. Your ticket number is 752."

Assuming the market is still above 101-00, your order will go into the floor broker's deck. Should prices move down to 101-00 and he can find a willing seller at that level, he will fill the trade for you.

Your broker will then call you back. "You bought two September bond futures at 101-00."

This is the time to place the stop. Knowing you want to risk just six ticks, you now give him the stop order. You don't tell him you want to place a stop-loss order six ticks below the market or the entry. You give him the specific price. The price of 101-00 represents 3232 when translated into 32nds. Six ticks below their number (3232 − 6 = 3226) is 100-26. You tell your broker: "For Account No. 23848, I want to sell two September bond contracts at 100-26 on a stop."

Now you will receive another ticket number. You now have a resting stop order below the market.

For your sake, hopefully the stop-loss order will not be hit. Rather, as anticipated, the market begins to rally, and soon it is trading at, let's say, 101-16, resulting in a half-basis-point profit. At this point, you may decide to place your exit order to take profits at your desired limit at 102-00.

You call your broker again. "This is John Jones. For Account No. 23848, I want to sell two September Treasury bond futures at 102 even, or better."

He repeats the order and gives you another ticket number.

Now the market must cooperate. If prices rise above 102-00, your sell order will be executed and you will have a $2,000 profit, minus commission fees. Since it is understood that most orders are good for the day only, you may then cancel your stop order if the market is trending higher, or simply allow it to expire at the end of the day's trading. If there is even a remote chance that the market might turn around and hit the stop, you must cancel the order. Otherwise, you will find yourself short two contracts at the stop—after you took profits.

If you want to be out at the end of the day regardless of price, you want to cancel both the stop order and the profit-taking order and exit via a market order. Each time you place an order, you want to write down the order. Then, if the order is executed, you want to make a note that the order was filled. Most traders keep a log of all their trades.

Here's a summary of what the broker needs to know:

1. Your name

2. Your account number

3. Whether you want to buy or sell

4. The number of contracts (1, 2, 6, 10, whatever)

5. The trading month (March, June, September, December, etc.)

6. The futures contract (U.S. Treasury bonds, S&P 500, Swiss francs, etc.)

7. The limit price, if any, or type of order (market, market on close, stop)

While confusing to new traders, order placement is very straightforward once you get the basics down. It is vitally important, however, that when you decide to get out you place the identical order, with one exception: If you initially bought, you must sell; if you initially sold, you must buy. For example, to get in, you might say:

"I want to *buy* one September bond futures at the market."

When the time comes to get out, you must *sell* the identical number of contracts with the same expiration month. So you would say:

"I want to *sell* one September bond futures at the market."

Whether you get in or out on a market or limit order is up to you. But the number of contracts, the contract month, and the futures must be the same. Not to confuse matters, but if you antic-ipate declining prices, you would initially sell short:

"I want to *sell* one September bond futures at the market."

When it comes time to get out, win or lose, you must *buy:*

"I want to *buy* one September bond futures at the market."

If you try selling when you are already short, you will simply add to the position.

If you are trading stocks, of course, you don't have to concern yourself with contract months. But, if you are trading options, you must add a number of qualifications to your order.

Do you want to buy or sell a put or a call? What is the name of the underlying stock or futures? What strike price option do you wish to buy or sell? Are you entering into an *opening* (new) or *closing* (old) transaction. Options are more complicated than stocks or futures; use extra caution when placing them. Your bro-kerage house will provide you with information on placing option orders.

33

Market on Close Orders: A Useful Exit Strategy

You will often get an excellent fill if you buy or sell to exit a position with a *market on close* order, known as a MOC order. Such orders are executed in the final minute of trading. As with any type of order, there are pros and cons to using this one.

Questions

What is the best type of market to use a MOC order? When should you place the order? What's the advantage to using a MOC order, versus a normal market order, 10 or 15 minutes prior to the close? Are MOC orders always filled? Why not hold a position overnight and get out on the open the following morning?

Answers

These are all good questions. They can help you create a winning exit strategy. MOC orders have the advantage of being filled in a moment of high liquidity. This means there typically are many buyers and sellers at the close. Whether you want to buy or sell, therefore, there will be someone to take the other side. The best time to enter a MOC order is 5 to 7 minutes prior to the close on a day when the market is trending. You also want to make sure you are using this order on a day on which you are on the winning side.

Why wait until just before the close to place the order? First, if you place the order more than 10 minutes prior to the close, the market may change direction. Then you will have to exit the market and call up your broker and cancel the MOC order. If you don't cancel in time, the order may be executed anyway, leaving you with an open position overnight. Second, if you wait too long (say 1 or 2 minutes prior to the close), the broker may not be able to get the order into the pit in time.

To understand why you want to be on the winning side of the trend, you have to understand the psychology at work in the market as you approach the close. The winning side is starting to squeeze the losing side. That means if prices are rising, the short-sellers are going to grow more panicked as prices continue to rise. This panic translates into emotional buying, anything to stem the growing losses. For the buyers, this means more profits as the short-sellers become emotional buyers to escape continued losses in the market overnight. If you are long, therefore, this scenario works for you. Get out MOC, selling into a mob of buyers. If the trend has been down, however, this works in the opposite fashion. Panicked buyers will only work to the advantage of the short-sellers by offering down the market as prices trend lower. The rule: If you are winning, wait for the close; if the trend is against you, get out before the close.

Going overnight involves taking on a lot more risk. The rule here is: Winning positions tend to improve in the overnight market, and losing positions tend to get worse. There are always exceptions, but why risk the exposure? If your perspective is long-term, going overnight is fine, assuming you understand the risks. Otherwise, cut your losses short by getting out well before the close.

Another time when it pays to avoid the close is when you have a choppy market. In the absence of a trend, the probabilities favor a move back to the middle, so holding on in hopes of a trend into the close doesn't make sense. Market on close orders are almost always filled. The only exception to this would be when you wait too late to place the order and get a busy signal from your broker. Once the closing bell rings, all trading must cease.

34

Limiting Losses:
When to Pull Back

It is not enough to place stops—mental or actual—to limit your losses in the market. You need to know when to place your cards on the table and get up and leave. So many trading disaster stories begin with a small loss. With time, the small loss grows larger, and soon the hapless trader is grasping at straws in a vain attempt to win at all costs. By that time, of course, it is already too late. So do yourself a favor and learn the warning signals.

Questions

What is the classic market pattern that is almost impossible to beat? How often does it occur? What should you do if repeated attempts to win are frustrated by the market? What do floor traders know about market patterns that goes unrecognized by the trading public? How do you adapt to changing market conditions?

Answers

To begin, you have to recognize that everyone has losing cycles in the market regardless of what he does. The idea is to minimize the negative impact of these cycles and to, indeed, expect them and learn to capitalize on them. Perhaps the most difficult market to trade is known as the *search-and-destroy* pattern. This occurs when the market repeatedly violates both the intraday highs and lows. For the aggressive trader, this pattern is especially problematic because his aggressiveness only serves to dig him in deeper. This pattern manifests itself when a whipsawing price pattern refuses to trend. In such an environment, getting aggressive only compounds the losses.

Ironically, you will find the search-and-destroy pattern in the market on two very distinct types of days—when nothing happens, and on report days when the news is subject to varying interpretation. Both can generate a whipsawing market, and both can defy conventional analysis. How do you make sense of random patterns? On the report days, you can do yourself a favor by waiting until the report is issued. Once the dust settles, you can begin to try to make sense of the price action. Just remember that market action is often the very opposite of what might be expected. One explanation for this behavior might be the old "buy the rumor, sell the news" market pattern. The market has risen on hopes of a bullish report. The report hits and the market declines. This would be an easy call if the market were cooperative, but on the heels of this news, the market might soar higher only to crash lower. How do you make sense of this? One suggestion is that you don't. You simply leave the report days alone until some sanity returns to the market.

The more classic search-and-destroy pattern often occurs not on the heels of the news, but in anticipation of it. So, if there is a report due tomorrow, most of the players will be on the sidelines. This leaves a narrow-range market that can be more easily manipulated one way or another. Even liquidity can be a problem in a market like this. One rule is to give it a shot three times. If you come up on the losing end on each one, walk away. It is not worth losing a major portion of your equity on one particularly bad day. Fortunately, this particular pattern is not all that prevalent. If you were to characterize every trading day, you would probably find that less than five percent of all trading days exhibit similar patterns.

Apart from knowing when to run, you need to have a strategy for coping with changing market conditions. If a market has just completed a major run higher, it needs time to consolidate before returning to its trending ways. That's when you have to rethink your strategy 180 degrees. For instance, if you have been winning on a consistent basis by buying breakouts, you'd do well to think about fading that strategy on a day when the market opens unchanged and shows very little directional trend. In day-of-the-week trading patterns, this is the quiet Tuesday morning following the barn-burner Monday rally. The market needs a break if only for three or four hours in the morning. Put another way, you want to do the very opposite on Tuesday morning of what you did on Monday morning. In this scenario, a Monday morning higher buy would be followed by a Tuesday morning higher sell. The simple reason is the market needs time to rest.

Cultivating this specific type of flexibility is a difficult challenge for most traders. However, if you are open to the experience, you might be able to make the transition from a more rigid approach. The goal, of course, is always the same: to limit losses while capitalizing on the genuine trends.

35

Slow Stochastics:
A Divergence Tool

Many traders use slow stochastics as a relative strength indicator. High readings suggest an overbought market and low readings suggest an oversold market. The problem with this approach, as with the bullish consensus, is that this indicator can get high—and stay high. The reverse is also true, of course, at market bottoms. If you are selling into a strong market, the premature selling may result in profits left on the table or, worse yet, a short position in a rising market. Better to use slow stochastics as a divergence tool, running them on a line chart below the one- or five-minute bars.

Question

Prices have been rising and profit-taking occurs. A clear-cut top is formed. Then prices rise to new highs. You consult your slow stochastics chart at the bottom of the screen. The first rally is matched identically by the slow stochastics chart. The second rally to new high ground, however, is not matched by slow stochastics. Rather, the second rally on the slow stochastics chart fails to rise to new highs. What is going on?

Answer

You have a reversal occurring. The second high on the price chart was probably the final high. The market is not returning to that price. The next trend, at least temporarily, is down. Get out immediately. The move is over. This is particularly true if the second rally in prices occurred over the same time period as the first rally. In this instance, the pattern was symmetrical in time, suggesting completion of the upward price pattern. When confirming indicators fail to match price patterns, they create a divergence. This is usually a sign that the move is over.